Published by Creative Education
123 South Broad Street, Mankato, Minnesota 56001
Creative Education is an imprint of The Creative Company

Art direction by Rita Marshall
Production design by The Design Lab

Photographs by Architect of the Capitol, Richard Cummins, Curator of the Supreme Court
(Franz Janssen), Hulton/Archive Photos (Lambert, New York Times/George Tames),
The Image Finders (Michael Evans, Patti McConville), National Archives and Records
Administration, North Wind Picture Archive, Ronald Reagan Library

Library of Congress Cataloging-in-Publication Data

Fitzpatrick, Anne, 1978–
The judicial system / by Anne Fitzpatrick.
p. cm. — (Let's investigate)
Summary: Introduces the judicial branch of the United States government and how it works.
ISBN 1-58341-263-8
1. Justice, Administration of—United States—Juvenile literature.
2. Courts—United States—Juvenile literature. 3. Judicial power—United
States—Juvenile literature. [1. Justice, Administration of. 2. Courts.
3. Judicial power.] I. Title. II. Series.
KF8700.Z9 F58   2003
347.73'1—dc21   2002034868

First edition

2 4 6 8 9 7 5 3 1

THE JUDICIAL SYSTEM

ANNE FITZPATRICK

Creative Education

JUDICIAL

C O S T

More than $3 million worth of marble was used in the construction of the Supreme Court building, which was completed in 1935.

What if there were no rules and everyone could do whatever he or she wanted? Sometimes it seems like people would be better off without laws, such as the law that says all kids must go to school. But what if a person wanted to go to school, but couldn't? The judicial branch of the United States government makes sure that laws protect freedom rather than restrict it.

Above, the Supreme Court building Right, pledging allegiance to the flag

JUDICIAL

PROTEST

Above, George Mason
Right, the United States Constitution

WHAT IS JUSTICE?

The people who wrote the **Constitution** of the United States in 1787 were very concerned about protecting freedom. They had just fought the American Revolutionary War to break away from the British government, which restricted their freedom. They decided to separate the powers of government into three branches, so that no one person or group of people would have the power to take freedom away.

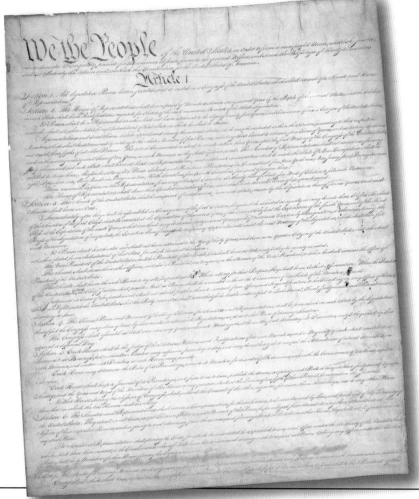

Justice is personified in paintings and statues as a blindfolded woman holding scales, to show that a judge must weigh each side of a case impartially.

Left, the courtroom of the Supreme Court of Pennsylvania Below, a statue symbolizing blind justice

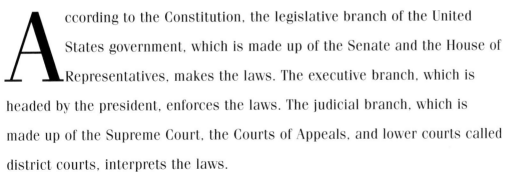

According to the Constitution, the legislative branch of the United States government, which is made up of the Senate and the House of Representatives, makes the laws. The executive branch, which is headed by the president, enforces the laws. The judicial branch, which is made up of the Supreme Court, the Courts of Appeals, and lower courts called district courts, interprets the laws.

JUDICIAL
FREEDOM

In 1989, the Supreme Court ruled that the state of Texas could not punish a man who burned an American flag because of the first amendment right to free speech.

The U.S. flag symbolizes the freedom and equality protected by the Constitution

The judicial branch does its job in three ways. It conducts **trials** of people who are accused of crimes and gives out **sentences** when they are found guilty. It tries to resolve disagreements among individuals, groups, or institutions. And it interprets the laws to make sure that they are being enforced in the way that the legislative branch intended and that they do not violate the Constitution.

What does it mean for a law to be just? Laws and the way they

are carried out must be **impartial**. All people must be treated the same way, whether they are rich or poor, black or white, male or female. Justice also involves making sure that people get what they deserve. When someone is accused of a crime, there must be very strong proof that he or she really did it and deserves to be punished. The punishment must also be just. Some crimes are worse than others and deserve harsher punishments.

JUDICIAL
CONDUCT

Judges must follow a Code of Conduct, which includes rules against engaging in politics and belonging to an organization that discriminates on the basis of sex, race, or religion.

When people give evidence in a trial, they must swear to tell the truth

JUDICIAL
R I G H T S

In 1966, in the case of Ernesto Miranda, who confessed to a crime without knowing his rights, the Supreme Court ruled that police must describe the fifth and sixth amendment rights before arresting someone.

Police officers must be careful not to violate a person's rights while making an arrest

A CITIZEN'S RIGHTS

The judicial branch protects the rights of every American citizen. It protects people from having crimes committed against them. It also protects people's freedom from being taken away unjustly. Ten changes, or amendments, were made to the Constitution in 1791. They are known as the Bill of Rights. Four of them protect the rights of citizens who are accused of a crime. These amendments are the basis of the American judicial system.

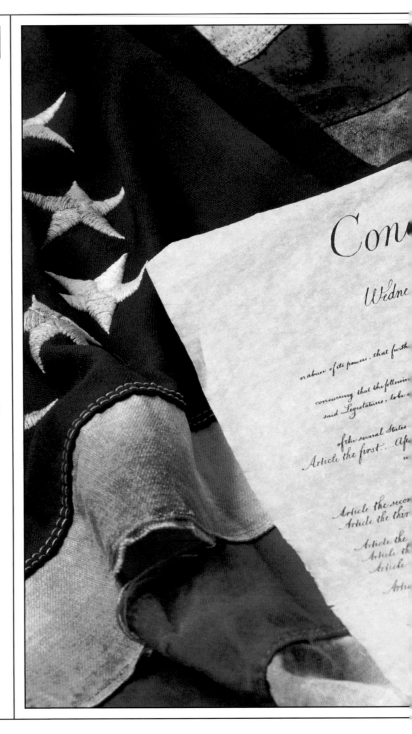

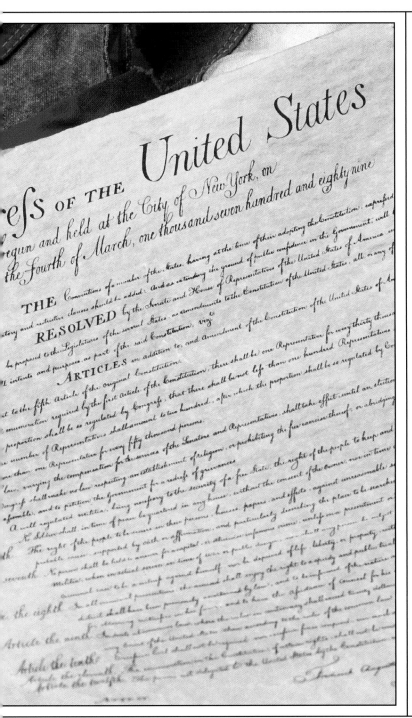

The fifth amendment states that a person cannot be forced to be a witness against himself or herself. If, by answering a question, a person would be admitting to a crime, he or she does not have to answer it. Instead, the person says that he or she "pleads the fifth."

JUDICIAL RULING

In 1943, the Supreme Court ruled it unconstitutional for a school to punish students who believed that it was against their religion to recite the Pledge of Allegiance to the American flag.

The Bill of Rights guarantees equal justice for all U.S. citizens

JUDICIAL
C A L L

he fifth amendment also describes the right of due process. This means that no citizen can be executed, imprisoned, or have property taken away without a trial. The right of due process ensures that Americans are considered innocent until proven guilty. The sixth and seventh amendments spell out how trials should be conducted so that the accused person will have every chance to defend himself or herself. The rights granted by these amendments include the right to a trial by jury, and the right to be represented in court by a lawyer.

It is important to be represented in a trial by someone who knows the law well

By 2002, there were 102 federal prisons in the United States, with more than 160,000 inmates. There were nearly two million inmates locked up in state and federal prisons.

13

T he eighth amendment protects citizens from "cruel and unusual punishments." After a person has been found guilty and sent to prison, he or she is still protected by the Constitution. The government is not allowed to torture a person, for example. Punishments for crimes are usually fines that must be paid, community service that must be carried out, or imprisonment for an appropriate length of time. Prisoners must be treated fairly. For example, they must be given enough food and receive medical care when needed.

Left, a prisoner serving his sentence
Above, prisons are well-guarded

JUDICIAL
TERMS

14

Lawyers may use pictures and videos to try to convince the jury

HOW IT WORKS

In criminal trials, the government is the **plaintiff** and accuses the **defendant** of breaking the law. Civil cases are disagreements among individuals or groups; the plaintiff **sues** the defendant for causing injury to the plaintiff or the plaintiff's property. A person injured in a car accident, for example, can sue the other driver for his or her injuries and the damage to his or her car.

Juries are selected from a group of people randomly drawn from lists of registered voters and licensed drivers. People who do not speak, read, and write English or who have been charged with a serious crime cannot be on a jury.

15

T he defendant can choose to have a trial by jury. A jury is a group of 12 ordinary citizens who listen to the case and decide whether the defendant is guilty or innocent. When there is no jury, a judge makes the decision. During a jury trial, the judge's role is to keep the trial running smoothly and instruct the jury on the laws that apply to the case.

Judges must pay close attention to everything that happens in a trial

JUDICIAL
CRIME

According to the Constitution, Congress can remove a justice from office only if he or she is found guilty of "Treason, Bribery, or other high Crimes and Misdemeanors."

Usually, each side has at least one lawyer to argue its case. A case is argued by presenting **evidence** to the judge or jury. Evidence might be documents or objects relating to a case or witnesses who can provide information about the case. The plaintiff's lawyer tries to convince the judge or jury that the defendant is guilty, and the defendant's lawyer tries to convince the judge or jury that the defendant is innocent.

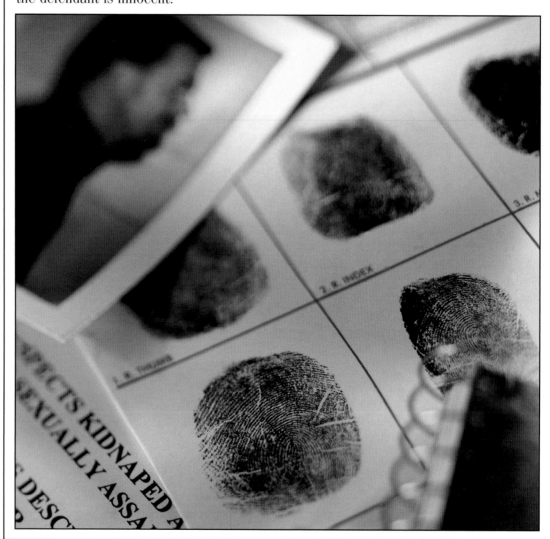

Fingerprints and witness identifications can be important evidence

The members of the jury discuss the case in private before announcing their decision. In a civil case, if they decide the defendant is guilty, the jury also decides on the amount of **damages** to be awarded. In a criminal trial, if the jury decides the defendant is guilty, the jury or judge decides on a sentence.

In a criminal trial, the judge may decide that the defendant does not have to stay in jail during the trial. The defendant gives the court a large amount of money, called bail, to guarantee that he or she will not run away.

17

The judge or jury decides whether a defendant is guilty or innocent

JUDICIAL
WORKLOAD

The Courts of Appeals were established in 1891, when the Supreme Court became overwhelmed by the number of appeals it was being asked to hear.

JUDICIAL
DECISIONS

Each year, the Supreme Court receives about 7,000 requests to hear an appeal, and it agrees to hear about 150. The justices usually do not reveal why they refuse to hear an appeal.

The courtroom of the United States Supreme Court

THE SUPREME COURT

Federal cases are held in a district court. There are 94 federal district courts in the United States, including at least one in each state. The 94 districts are divided into 12 circuits, each of which has a Court of Appeals. A defendant or plaintiff can ask the Court of Appeals to hear his or her case if the judgment of the court seems unfair. If the Court of Appeals refuses to hear the case, or if the defendant or plaintiff thinks that its judgment is also

unfair, then an **appeal** is made to the United States Supreme Court. Each state also has its own judicial system, including a state supreme court to which cases can be appealed.

JUDICIAL
APPEAL

A panel of three judges hears each case brought before an Appeals Court. An appeal cannot be heard by a jury.

JUDICIAL
LOCATION

Before the court-house of the Supreme Court was built in Washington, D.C., the Court once heard cases in a tavern because it had no other place to meet.

JUDICIAL

SEATING

The chief justice of the Supreme Court sits at the center of a long table at the front of the Court's chamber, and the most senior justices sit closest to him or her.

JUDICIAL

PAY

According to the Constitution, neither Congress nor the president can reduce the amount that a justice is paid. In 2002, the salary of the chief justice was $192,600, and the other justices' salaries were $184,400.

The conference room where the Supreme Court meets to discuss cases

Every Wednesday afternoon, the nine justices, or judges, of the federal Supreme Court hold a private meeting to discuss requests for appeals and vote on which cases to hear. In order for a case to be heard by the Supreme Court, four or more justices must vote for it. If the case is not accepted, the judgment of the lower court stands.

JUDICIAL

Every time the Supreme Court meets, each justice shakes hands with each of the other eight justices. The tradition reminds them that although they may have different opinions, they have one purpose.

JUDICIAL
WISDOM

The wise judge King Solomon of ancient Israel once ordered that a baby two women claimed as their own be cut in half, knowing the real mother would give in first.

The Supreme Court sets time limits for lawyers' arguments

The justices must also decide whether to hear new arguments in a case, or to simply review the arguments already made in the lower courts. When the Supreme Court hears new arguments in a case, the lawyers on each side get only 30 minutes each to present their argument. Most of the justices' time is spent researching the laws and **precedents** that apply to the case. A justice must base his or her decision on laws, the Constitution, and decisions made by other judges. A decision cannot be based on the justice's personal views or feelings.

O nce they have read all information and heard all arguments, the justices meet to discuss and vote on the case. The opinion of the greatest number of justices determines how the Court will rule. If most of the justices think that the ruling of the lower court was correct and fair, the appeal is denied and the lower court's ruling stands. If most of the justices think that the lower court's decision may not have been correct or fair, they can either change the decision or send the case back to the lower court for reconsideration.

Since it was established in 1789, the Supreme Court has struck down all or part of more than 1,000 state laws and about 125 federal laws.

The U.S. Supreme Court in 2002

JUDICIAL
CHANGE

Originally, there were six justices on the Supreme Court. The number changed seven times before it settled at nine in 1869.

JUDICIAL
DUTIES

In the early years of the Supreme Court, the justices had to travel around the country hearing cases. It was a grueling job that few people wanted.

Judges bang a gavel, or wooden hammer, to call for silence in the courtroom

The chief justice chooses one of the justices on the side of the majority to write the **majority opinion**. In this document, he or she describes why the court thinks the way it does. Any justice who disagreed with the majority can write a **dissent**, in which he or she describes his or her reasons for disagreeing. All opinions are made available to the public and permanently

stored in the Court's records. The opinions of the Supreme Court can change the way laws are applied. The Court can even decide that a law is unfair or **unconstitutional** and should therefore no longer be enforced.

JUDICIAL
OUTRAGE

In one infamous decision that was later reversed, the Supreme Court of 1857 ruled that Dred Scott, a slave, did not have the right to sue his owner because he was property, not a person.

25

Dred Scott was an important figure in the history of the Supreme Court

JUDICIAL
HISTORY

Lawyer Thurgood Marshall argued Linda Brown's case against the Topeka school board in front of the Supreme Court. He became the first African-American Supreme Court justice in 1967.

Earl Warren was chief justice of the Supreme Court from 1953 to 1969

JUSTICE IS BLIND

In 1951, a young black girl named Linda Brown wanted to go to the all-white school in her neighborhood in Topeka, Kansas. In Kansas at that time, black children and white children were not allowed to attend school together. Linda Brown and her parents sued the school board of Topeka, and the case went all the way to the federal Supreme Court. In the majority opinion, Chief Justice Earl Warren wrote, "Separate educational facilities are inherently unequal." It was the first

of many Supreme Court decisions that ruled that the law must protect all races equally, changing earlier decisions and laws.

The writers of the Constitution knew that people in power cannot always be trusted to do the right thing. They tried to make sure that there is always a chance for ordinary people to change an unfair law or court ruling. Appealing to the Supreme Court, as Linda Brown and her parents did, is one of the most important ways that this can be done.

There have been 16 chief justices in the history of the Supreme Court. The first was John Jay, appointed in 1789.

John Jay served as chief justice of the Supreme Court for five years

JUDICIAL

AGE

In 2002, the youngest Supreme Court justice was Clarence Thomas, who was 53. Justice John Paul Stevens was the oldest, at 81.

JUDICIAL

SUPPORT

Each Supreme Court justice has four assistants, called clerks. They are usually people who have recently graduated from law school. The clerks help the justice research, or study, each case.

Chief Justice Warren Burger swearing in Ronald Reagan as president

Supreme Court justices are not elected like the president or members of Congress. Justices and other federal judges are nominated by the president, and the Senate votes to confirm the appointment. Once they are confirmed, Supreme Court justices can serve as long as they want. Although the appointment and confirmation of a justice is sometimes political, the justice cannot be affected by politics once confirmed. This protects the judicial branch of the U.S. government from political bias (personal feelings).

JUDICIAL

EQUALITY

In 1981, Sandra Day O'Connor became the first woman on the Supreme Court. The Senate confirmed her appointment by a vote of 99–0.

Sandra Day O'Connor being sworn in as a Supreme Court justice

JUDICIAL
TENURE

The longest-serving justice of the Supreme Court was William O. Douglas. He remained a justice for more than 36 years, from 1938 to 1975.

The Constitution ensures that the judicial branch has the independence to be impartial. It also ensures that the interpretation of laws can change as the needs of citizens change. Each case that comes before a court is examined individually, and laws are interpreted as they apply to a particular case. Citizens of the United States can feel safe knowing that the law is made by and for them.

The Supreme Court building embodies the power of the judiciary

Glossary

An **appeal** is a request that a higher court review a lower court's decision to make sure it is just.

The **Constitution** is the document that outlines the United States government and how it works.

The amount of money that a plaintiff must pay to a defendant in a civil case is called **damages**.

A **defendant** is the person accused of a crime in a criminal case, or the person being sued in a civil case.

In a **dissent**, justices who disagree with the majority opinion write an explanation of their views.

Information presented to a judge or jury to convince them to rule one way or the other is called **evidence**.

Something is described as **federal** when it refers to the government of the whole United States, rather than a state government.

To be **impartial** is to not be influenced by previously formed opinions and prejudices.

A **majority opinion** is a written explanation of the decision made by the court.

The person who files the complaint in a civil case is called the **plaintiff**.

Precedents are decisions made in earlier cases that influence a court's ruling.

Sentences are punishments, usually a certain amount of time in prison, that courts order for guilty defendants.

A plaintiff **sues** a defendant by asking a court of law to make the defendant pay for harm caused to the plaintiff.

Trials are investigations into the facts of a case in order to prove that a defendant is guilty or innocent.

A law that conflicts with some part of the Constitution is called **unconstitutional**.

Index